SHURMON CLARKE & DEANA WILLIAMSON

WESTBOW
PRESS®
A DIVISION OF THOMAS NELSON
& ZONDERVAN

Cover Design by
Reginald Simmons (Imagine Graphics, Freeport, Bahamas-reggiesimmons@gmail.com)
Printed in the USA
Graphics by
123rf.com
Illustration placement by
Shurmon Clarke/Westbow Press
Edited by
Evelyn Pinder-Dames, Courtney Cunningham, Sharon Greene
Also used www.grammarly.com

Scripture quotations marked NLT are taken from the Holy Bible, New Living Translation. *New Living Translation* copyright ©1996, 2004, 2007, 2013, 2015 by Tyndale House Foundation. Used by permission of Tyndale House Publishers Inc., Carol Stream, Illinois 60188. All rights reserved.

WestBow Press books may be ordered through booksellers or by contacting:

WestBow Press
A Division of Thomas Nelson & Zondervan
1663 Liberty Drive
Bloomington, IN 47403
www.westbowpress.com
1 (866) 928-1240

ISBN: 978-1-9736-1799-0 (sc)
ISBN: 978-1-9736-1800-3 (e)

Library of Congress Control Number: 2018902210

Print information available on the last page.

WestBow Press rev. date: 5/11/2018

DEDICATION

SHURMON CLARKE

To God who has created, gifted and sustains me through my life's journey.

To my mother, Carolyn Evans, who introduced me to God, the church and first believed in my potential.

To my father, James Thompson who taught me the value of knowledge and education.

To my family: Wendal (husband) and my children, Wendal Jr, Jayvyn and Madison, my three most precious gifts from God.

To Pastor, C. J. Beckles for teaching me the beauty and power of studying God's word and helped me to discover my 'strengths' (*www.gallupstrengthscenter.com*).

To my Pastor Glen C. Russell and my friend, Ruby Pinder for assisting and providing me with the platform to discover my instinct and destiny.

To the mentors, coaches, teachers, advisors God placed in my life to influence and helped me whether directly or indirectly to realize my potential, my gifts, provide knowledge and training, and help me discover God's purposes for my life. Some of these mentors and coaches are Sonovia Hanna (*my spiritual mother*), Laquita Collie, Sharon Greene, Evelyn Pinder-Dames, Billie Bowe, Randy Thompson, Larry Kelly, Michael Hyatt, Priscilla Shirer, Beth Moore, Dr. Myles Munroe, Bishop T.D. Jakes and John Maxwell.

To Team Bain (Body-4-EVER), my exercise trainers, who taught me the value of discipline, self-control, proper mindset and accountability ("fill your cup" and "to own it").

To my sisters (Monique, Michelle, Athina, Alexis and Karis), brothers (Kieyros, Kwasi and Jason), other family members and friends (*confidantes, constituents and comrades*) especially Torry, Ruby, Ruth and Deana who support, listen, advise, encourage and pray for me. Thank you all so much.

DEANA GLINTON-WILLIAMSON

To my one and only Heavenly Father who has graciously allowed me to still be here on the face on this earth, I say thank you. Words are not enough to express my gratitude.

To my earthly dad, Wesley Glinton, who always taught me to never settle for mediocrity, and to speak up for injustice whenever possible. You're accredited for my tenacious spirit.

To my one and ONLY child, Alexander Rasheed, you are my special gift from God, and my number one fan. You compel me to be the best that I can be. Continue to check me.

To my mother, Angeline Glinton, who showed me all my life that it is better to give than to receive. She's responsible for my giving spirit.

To all my sisters and other relatives, friends like siblings, and my pastor, C.J. Beckles, who have supported me in being myself, I love you for letting me be me! Thank you all.

CONTENTS

ABOUT THE AUTHORS

SHURMON CLARKE

Shurmon Clarke is a teacher, mentor, parent, leader, trainer and aspiring life coach. With a Master's degree in Chemistry and undergraduate degrees in the areas of Science and Law, she enjoys the pursuit of knowledge and wisdom as well as counseling, mentoring, coaching, training and teaching. Shurmon is passionate about helping people discover the gifts that God has deposited in them. She is also excited about the process of personal and professional growth.

She is a former College Lecturer and currently works in the field of Human Resources within the Pharmaceutical manufacturing industry. Shurmon is currently serving as a volunteer leader at her local church and has been serving faithfully in various ministry roles over the past twenty years.

She is growing as a Christian woman, wife and the parent of three wonderful and gifted children, Wendal Jr, Jayvyn, and Madison. In her rest time (pit stops), she enjoys reading, studying the Bible, gathering knowledge, exercising, meditation, sports and watching movies.

Please feel free to contact her at lifeskills101therace@gmail.com

DEANA GLINTON-WILLIAMSON

Deana is a former Teacher of the Year for a large public primary school on the island of Grand Bahama. She has a B. Sc. Degree in Elementary Education and a Master of Arts in Curriculum & Instructions K-12. Deana humbly serves her community through her local Kiwanis Club and has been awarded the title of Distinguished President by Kiwanis International.

She has spent her career in both the pharmaceutical industry and in the field of education for over 25 years. Deana is also a co-founder of BahamasEducationExpress.com which is an online educational website that assists teachers and students with educational materials pertinent to The Bahamas.

Deana writes essays, papers, articles, and Gospel tracts. She also enumerates surveys, develops curricula, speaks at small groups, and consults part-time. She also enjoys researching, problem-solving, listening to classical music, bird watching, and ministering to others ("my things.") She is a single mother of one.

Please feel free to contact her at williamson.deana@gmail.com

LIFE'S RACE

"Study this Book of Instruction continually. Meditate on it day and night so you will be sure to obey everything written in it. Only then will you prosper and succeed in all you do.."
(Joshua 1:8 NLT)

As a teenager, this is a pivotal point in your life. You are moving and developing from the stage of childhood to adulthood. This journey is basically a race and is comparable to a car race. The starting line for the voyage is birth, and there is a limited time to complete the race or journey. To be successful in life's race, as in car racing, you will need several critical components which include: a driver, a team, and a Team Leader. Whom you choose for the position of Team Leader is significant. The Team Leader will determine your level of success, how you manage yourself during your race, and how you end. Also for your race, you will learn about your self-worth and skills as the driver, identify your team members, determine the required resources, learn about utilizing pit stops, about money management and how rules and authorities should govern your life.

The purpose of *Life Skills 101: The Race* is to teach you over 8-weeks of interactive study sessions, how to successfully navigate one's life track using seven (7) basic life principles and skills. The series uses the analogy between the sport of car racing and our life's journey to explain the principles and skills given in each lesson. The last session (8th week) is a review of the previous seven lessons. These principles and skills will help you navigate your journey and teach you how to make wise choices, deal with disappointments and handle unfavorable conditions or challenges that you will face on your journey. Additionally, these principles and skills will hopefully assist you in avoiding unnecessary mistakes, decisions, and failures.

The foundation of these principles and skills is the Word of God. Knowing God (your Team Leader), having a relationship with God, and practically applying His word is the basis of a successful life's race.

HOW TO USE

This workbook contains the weekly lessons, group sessions, and the personal assignments (challenges). Each session consists of a video or PowerPoint lesson followed by a group session and then a personal challenge. The video or PowerPoint section is designed to be viewed at the beginning of each session. Please do your best to complete the personal challenges. These are intended to reinforce the concepts and principles from the video or PowerPoint and group sessions. This training can be done in a group setting or as a personal study. Once you have completed all eight lessons, you would have learned about several life skills and principles that will help you navigate your life's race.

SELFIE

Complete the following questions about you, if possible add a 'selfie' photo of yourself.

Name:

_____

Date of Birth:

_____

High School:

_____

Church:

Add Photo here

_____

Favorite Meal:

_____

Are You a Christian?:

_____

Favorite TV show:

_____

List your top three friends:

_____

Favorite School Subjects:

_____

Favorite Song/Artist:

_____

List your top three life and career goals?

_____

_____

_____

_____

Do you want to live a successful life?

_____

Describe yourself in five sentences below:

_____

_____

_____

_____

_____

_____

```
                    Start....


                              Lesson#1

                              Big Idea-The driver needs a
                              Team Leader


            Lesson#2

    Big Idea- The driver must know their self-worth and
    possess the required skills


                              Lesson#3

                              Big Idea-The driver needs a team


                              Lesson#4

                              -Big Idea-The driver must manage money well


            Lesson#5

    Big Idea-The driver needs to take pit stops during the race


            Lesson#6

    Big Idea-The driver must be govern by rules and authorities


                              Lesson#7

                              Big Idea-The driver needs resources for the race


                    .....Finish
```

START......

LESSON #1

TEAM LEADER

TEAM LEADER

"Everything rises and falls on leadership."
-John C. Maxwell

INTRODUCTION

In car racing, there are three main characters: The Team Leader, the Driver, and the Racing Team. The Team Leader is the most important character and plays the most important role on the team. The Team Leader determines the plan, the outcome and the success of the team. The Team Leader can achieve this through influencing the team, associated persons and the system. Of course, this impacts the driver, the team, and the race.

The role of the Team Leader for your life is just as important as it is in car racing. Whom you choose for this position will impact the success of your life's race.

Success does not mean money! Remember that money cannot buy true happiness. Wealth, not money, encompasses having ways to provide for one's responsibilities, having good health, clarity of thought, great relationships, and peace of mind. This, my friend, is real success; and it starts with having the right Team Leader for your life, and that leader is none other than God!

In this lesson, we will identify the role and responsibilities of the Team Leader, select the best Team Leader for your life's race based on the possible choices and learn about vision and race strategy.

#CHECK THIS OUT!

"How great you are, O Sovereign LORD ! There is no one like you.
We have never even heard of another God like you!."
(2 Samuel 7:22 NLT)

#PRESS PLAY

Watch the Video or PowerPoint Lesson on ***Team Leader.*** Follow and fill in the blanks in your workbook. Feel free to jot down any points, quotes, or ideas that have impacted you.

THE TEAM LEADER

THE TEAM LEADER:

1. Has the _____ for the driver, the team, and the race and is in control of the driver and team.

2. Develops _____ for the driver, the team and the race based on their vision.

3. Develops the _____ for the race based on the vision and goals.

4. _____ and _____ the team.

5. Is _____ as well as _____ about the driver, racing conditions, the car, the rules, and the racing organization.

6. Knows the _____ of the car and selects the car for the races.

7. _____ to execute the race plan and _____ the talents, skills, personality style, limitations, and knowledge of the _____.

8. _____ the driver and team and the associated activities before, during and after the race.

9. Is _____ for the outcome of the races.

10. Makes_____ for the driver and the racing team.

The possible options for the role of Team Leader for your life's race are:

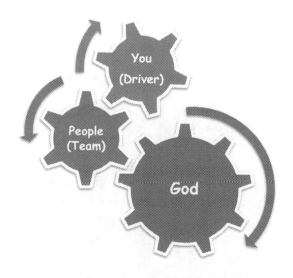

Life Skills 101: The Race

|Equipping Teenagers with the skills that they will need to make wise choices and navigate a successful life's race|

OPTION#1 -GOD

The dictionary (dictionary.com) defines God as *"the creator and ruler of the universe and source of all moral authority; the supreme being, a superhuman being or spirit worshipped as having power over nature or human fortunes; a deity."* Let's look at the nature and characteristics of God and then, we will compare God to the other options to see whether God is the best choice for the role of Team Leader for your life's race.

God is known by his names, nature, characteristics, and activities in the Bible. Therefore let's look at some of the nature and characteristics of God:

1. God is all _____(Omnipotent). *Psalms 21:13*

2. God knows _____ (Omniscient). *Proverbs 3:19*

3. God is _____ (Omnipresent). *Jeremiah 23:24*

4. _____ (name of God) who created _____. *Genesis 1*

5. Yahweh (name of God) is the _____personal God. *Exodus 3: 13-15*

6. Jehovah Jireh (name of God) means _____. *Genesis 22:14*

7. God is also called our _____ and _____. *Psalms 47:6-8, Psalms 23:1*

8. God is _____. *Revelations 1:4*

9. God created a _____and _____ for your life. *Jeremiah 29:11*

10. Jehovah Nissi (name of God) means _____ (God fights my battles). *Exodus 17:8-15*

OPTION#2 -THE DRIVER

The driver is another key member of the team. The driver navigates the car around the track during the race using the plan designed by the Team Leader.

Instructions and directions are given by the Team Leader to the driver before, during and after the contest.

The driver is dependent on his/her team members before the race, during the pit stops, and after the races. Although the driver appears in the winner's circle and answers to the press, the decisions related to the car, driver selection, sponsorship and the team are all the responsibilities of the Team Leader.

THE DRIVER:

1. The driver is _____ to the car during the race.

2. The driver is limited to what he or she can _____ during the race.

3. The driver's _____ and _____ is limited based on his or her observations during the race.

4. The driver is _____ with the ability and resources to address or solve the problem when there are _____ with the car or adverse racing conditions.

OPTION#3 -TEAM MEMBERS

In car racing, there are many different types of team members, and they play many different roles.

Before the race, the Engineers design the car.

During the race, the pit crew sustains the driver and maintains the car during the pit stops.

Also, equally important, are the administrative team members who are responsible for managing all of the administrative functions of the team.

For your life's race, you will also need a team of individuals that play various different roles.

1. The team members are _____ to their designated positions during the race, their sight and viewpoint are limited.

2. The team members _____ is limited to what they can control during the race.

3. The team members' _____ and vision are limited based on their position, roles and observations during the race.

4. The team members are _____ to their ability and resources to address or solve the problem when there are _____ with the car or adverse racing conditions,.

5. The team members for your life will consist of _____, _____, _____, _____, _____ and _____.

VISION/DREAMS

1. Visions are _____, _____of things that you want to accomplish during your life's race.

2. You should have _____and _____ for your life.

3. God gives us _____and _____ for our lives

4. To achieve your dreams and visions, they must be developed into _____ and a _____.

"When people do not accept divine guidance, they run wild. But whoever obeys the law is joyful." (Proverbs 29:18 NLT)

RACE STRATEGY/PLAN

1. The race car driver _____ the car around the track using the plan and guidance of the Team Leader.

2. The _____of your race experience is dependent upon your choice of the roles of Team Leader.

3. Your race strategy will consist of a _____, _____ and _____for the critical areas of your life.

4. Allow God (Team Leader) to guide and direct all areas of your life (<u>health</u>, <u>money</u>, _____, _____, _____, _____ and _____) during your life's race.

#GROUP CHAT

Take 10-15 minutes to answer the questions below in your workbook and then discuss your answers with your group:

Exercise#1: Answer the following question about God

What do you believe about God?

_____

_____

_____

_____

Exercise#2: Answer the following question about the driver

If the driver plays the role of Team Leader, what challenges would the driver and team face before during and after the race?

_____

_____

_____

_____

Exercise#3: Answer the following question about team members

If the team member plays the role of Team Leader, what challenges would the driver and team face before during and after the race?

_____

_____

_____

_____

Exercise#4: Complete the following table by selecting (with a 'x') the best option for carrying out each requirement. Then total the number of 'x' for each option and determine which option has the highest score.

Team Leader (Requirements)	God	You	People
Selecting the driver and the team.			
Developing and orchestrating a strategic plan for the race			
Choosing, assigning, guiding and training the driver, the car and the team.			
Knows the detail design, experience, knowledge, and skills of the car, driver and team members.			
Knows the talents, strengths, personality style, limitations and skills of the driver.			
Guides, direct, instruct, manages and advise driver and the team before, during and after the races.			
Is able to see the actions/activities and the racing conditions during the race and make necessary critical decisions especially during adverse conditions.			
Total			

Which of the above options has the highest total based on your selection?

_____

Exercise#5: Write down in the space below what you would like to see for your life in the following categories:

Health

_____

_____

_____

_____

Job/Career

_____

_____

_____

Relationship with God (Team Leader)

_____

_____

_____

_____

Marriage/Family

_____

_____

_____

_____

Friends

_____

_____

_____

_____

Finances

_____

_____

_____

_____

Education or Business

_____

_____

_____

_____

#GROUP PRAYER

End your study session with a prayer based on the skills and principles taught from the lesson.

#PERSONAL CHALLENGE

During the upcoming week complete the following challenge by answering the following questions:

Question#1: Is God the Team Leader of your life?

Yes ☐

No ☐

Question#2: If your answer above is no, are you interested in making God, the Team Leader of your life?

Yes ☐

No ☐

If your answer to question #2 above is yes, please follow the instructions below for the process to make God the Team Leader of your Life's Race.

Steps (How to become a Christian):

A –Admit that you are a sinner, repent and turn from your sin. *(Romans 3:23, Romans 6:23, Acts 3:19).*

B- Believe that Jesus is the son of God and accept God's gift of forgiveness for your sin. *(Romans 5:8, Acts 4:12, John 3:16).*

C- Confess your faith in Jesus Christ as your Savior and Lord. (*Romans 10:9-10, 13*)

Adapted from Lifeway (http://www.lifeway.com/Article/
Becoming-a-Christian-can-be-as-easy-as-A-B-C)

Question#3: If your answer to question#2 was yes, did you follow the process above, accepted and made God the Team Leader of your life's race?

Yes ⬜

No ⬜

"Even the righteousness of God which is by faith of Jesus Christ unto all and upon all them that believe: for there is no difference:" *(Romans 3:22 KJV)*

Note:

Whatever choice you make for Team Leader (in lesson#1), please continue with the others sessions to determine how your choice for this critical role fits in with the other areas of your life's journey that will be discussed.

LESSON #2

THE DRIVER

THE DRIVER

"Others can inspire you, but ultimately the only thing that empowers you is what lies within you and learning how to better utilize what you've been given."
— T.D. Jakes

INTRODUCTION

In car racing, the car driver is equipped and skill to perform the role of navigating the car around the track during the race. The Team Leader selects the driver based on their skills, talents, personality, experience, knowledge, and passion that they possess. The driver follows a plan designed by the Team Leader. The driver submits to and relies on the wisdom and direction of the Team Leader before, during and after the race. The success of the driver is dependent on his or her ability to carry out the plan designed by the Team Leader.

As, the driver for your life's race you are equipped with skills, talents, knowledge, passions, personality styles. God, the Team Leader, created you for a purpose and a plan. It is your responsibility to discover what God has equipped you with and utilize those gifts for the purposes he has for your life.

During your life's race, God's plans and purpose for your life may include writing books, making significant scientific discoveries, inventing things, developing businesses and creating artistic masterpieces. These activities could heal, deliver, transform and impact many people. To fully understand your purpose, you need to choose the right Team Leader and connect to the right Team Leader. Additionally, submit to the strategic plan the Team Leader has for your life. Your success during your life's race is dependent on your abilities God has given to you to fulfill the plan designed for you.

In this lesson, you will identify the role and responsibilities of the driver, the importance of self-worth and the skills that you the driver needs for your life's race.

#CHECK THIS OUT!

"Thank you for making me so wonderfully complex! Your workmanship is marvelous—how well I know it." (Psalms 139:14 NLT)

#PRESS PLAY

Watch the Video or PowerPoint Lesson on **The Driver.** Follow and fill in the blanks in your workbook. Feel free to jot down any points, quotes, or ideas that have impacted you.

THE DRIVER

The race car driver is one of the most highly conditioned athletes in the world. This sport requires a high level of demand for stamina and endurance. Therefore, the driver must have the right conditioning, skills, talents, personality, experience, and knowledge to carry out this role.

Similarly, for your life's race, there will be challenges, critical decisions that must be made and curves (*some expected and other unexpected*). Therefore, you too must be conditioned, possess stamina, endurance and have the required skills, talents, personality, experience, knowledge for your journey.

DRIVER-RESPONSIBILITIES

1. Takes the _____, _____ and _____ of the Team Leader and _____ it on the track.

2. Communicates with the _____ and _____ of the team about the state and performance of the car continually during the race. The Team Leader then determines which adjustments are needed.

3. Must possess the _____, _____, _____, _____ and abilities.

4. Must also have good _____, _____, _____ and _____.

5. Must be _____, _____, _____ and _____.

6. Must invest the _____, _____ and _____ to be good at his sport.

DRIVER-IDENTITY (ID)

The driver must have confidence in their ability to complete the race successfully. It is important to the driver that the Team Leader who selects him believes in his potential and ability to navigate and completes the race successfully. The driver must have a healthy self-worth (Identity-ID).

All human beings have a natural need to feel respected, accepted, and valued (self-worth). Robert S. McGee in his book "*The Search for Significance*" defines self-worth or personal significance "*as a quiet sense of self-respect and a feeling of satisfaction with who you are*"

You can have a healthy or an unhealthy view or comfort with who you are. An unhealthy view can lead to a feeling of being inferior, weak and helpless.

Developing a healthy self-worth is a critical skill needed for realizing your potential and destiny for your life's race. It is important that you learn to see yourself how God (Team Leader) sees you based on your relationship with him.

1. You can base your self-esteem or self-worth on the _____ view or the _____ view.

2. The cultural view or mindset defines or measures self-worth based on _____ and what other people _____ about the person (opinion).

3. The biblical view defines self-worth base on what _____.

CULTURAL VIEW

Robert McGee in his book "*The Search for Significance*" provides four areas that demonstrates the cultural viewpoint of self -worth or self-esteem. These areas are as follows:

- Performance

- Approval

- Blame

- Shame

Let's review these and compare those to God's view of self -worth or self-esteem based on a relationship with Jesus Christ.

1. PERFORMANCE

When a person believes that they must meet a _____ to feel good about themselves.

(Therefore this person is often driven to succeed, to prove that they are not a failure or they withdraw to avoid failure).

2. APPROVAL

When a person believes that they must be _____ to feel good about themselves.

(Therefore this person often fears rejection, loneliness, gives in to peer pressure, can be over sensitive to criticism and may demonstrate extreme people pleasing, etc.).

3. BLAME

When a person believes that whenever _____, they are _____ and therefore deserves _____.

(Therefore this person often fears punishment, blame others for their actions, can be defensive of their actions and will often take steps to avoid failure).

4. SHAME

When a person believes that they are who they are, that they _____ change and therefore are _____.

(Therefore this person feels shame, hopeless, inferior, often views himself as a victim, often withdraw from others or does actions that they think will bring significance).

GOD'S VIEW

God made you a unique (one of a kind), intricate, original, fearfully and wonderfully made human being. There is no one like you on this earth! Additionally, God the creator, all mighty King and Lord desires an intimate relationship or connection with you!

You can enter into that relationship with God (Team Leader) through acceptance of His son Jesus Christ (as your personal savior). This link gives a new identity in Jesus Christ now based on how God sees you.

Let's look at how our new ID in Jesus Christ helps you to fight against the false cultural beliefs discussed above.

1. When I accept Jesus my sins are forgiven and I became totally pleasing to God.
(*Romans 5:1*)

2. When I accept Jesus Christ I enter into a relationship with him and God forever. I am totally accepted by God.
(*Col 1:21-22*)

3. God sent Jesus Christ to died on the cross, he satisfied the penalty for my sins. I became God's child, deeply, forever and unconditionally loved by *God*
(*1 John 4:9-11*)

4. When I accept Jesus I became a new person with new abilities and I am complete in Jesus Christ
(*John 3:3-6*)

WHO ARE U?

*My feelings or internal needs should not be based on **skills**, **performance or people's opinion** but that my Team Leader (God) **loves, accepts** and **forgives without any conditions**.*

THE DRIVER-SKILLS

The gifts that God has placed in you to be successful in your life's race are:

- Personality
- Talents
- Skills
- Passions
- Knowledge

PERSONALITY

1. Your personality is the sum total of your _____, _____, _____ and _____ characteristics.

2. It exposes how you _____, _____, feels and _____ with others.

3. There is no _____ or _____ personality.

4. Learn to _____, _____ and use the personality that God blessed you with.

TALENT & SKILLS

1. A Talent is a natural _____ (innate). Therefore they were given to us by _____ (*Romans 12:6*).

2. It is something you do. Naturally, you just do without _____ about it.

3. Our talents were given by _____ to _____ others (*1 Peter 4:10*).

4. Everyone has some _____

5. A skill is the ability to do something with some level of _____.

6. A skill can be _____ or _____ through training or experience (*Exodus 35;36*).

Examples of some talents/skills are:

List of Skills & Talents		
Critical Thinking	Listening	Self-Discipline
Decision Making	Typing	Encouraging
Accounting	Imaginative	Learner
Marketing	Analyzing the past	Sign Language
Advertising	Inspiring	Teaching / Training
Graphic design	Story Telling	Negotiating Skills
Music	Communication Skills	Leadership
Art	Project Management	Managing

Computers (design, software, and hardware)	Sales	Organizing/Planning
Drawing	Problem Solving	Connecting with Others
Photography	Conflict Resolution	Coaching
Woodworking	Foreign Language	Mentoring
Programming	Adaptability	Analytical
Jokes / Humor	Athleticism	Decorating
Creativity	Empathy	Pioneering
	Knowledge	Researching
	Performing/Acting	

PASSION

YOUR PASSION:

1. Is related to things and activities that you _____ to do and the challenges that we feel an urge to solve.

2. Ignites your _____ and _____ you to act.

    "So Moses summoned Bezalel and Oholiab and all the others who were specially gifted by the LORD and were eager to get to work." (Exodus 36:2 NLT)

KNOWLEDGE

1. This is the awareness or _____ of something or someone gain through experience or education.

2. This includes facts, _____ and skills.

3. There are also academic subjects where you have acquired the most _____ and can possibly _____ or provide guidance to others.

#GROUP CHAT

Take 10-15 minutes to answer the questions below in your workbook and then discuss your answers with your group:

Exercise#1: Answer the following questions

Describe yourself in 2-3 sentences?

_____

_____

_____

Are you satisfied with who you are or how you see yourself?

_____

_____

_____

Do you struggle with the cultural traps of performance, approval, shame or blame based on the lesson? _____

Based on your area of struggle identified by your response above, write out what is the biblical solution given from the lesson.

_____

_____

_____

Exercise#2: Answer the following question

Based on the table above write out some of your talent and skills God has blessed you with.

_____

_____

_____

Exercise#3: Your Facilitator will allow you to take the Personality Assessment. After completing the assessment write in the space below your top two personality styles. Then, using the personality styles descriptions below talk about your results with your group.

_____

_____

Social Styles Personality Styles Descriptions

Driver-*Highly focused on achieving goals; often not concerned with the relationships around them due to tunnel vision on accomplishing goals. Task focused rather than people focused. Often competitive and measure themselves by achieving results or accomplishments.*

Analytical-*like to think things through logically; they need details such as numbers and facts; are concerned with the truth and accuracy. Task focused rather than people focused. They like to be right and will often not make a decision until they have all the facts.*

Amiable-*like steadiness; love harmony and peace; their focus is on relationships and the feelings of others; they are people oriented. People focused rather than task focused. They have a challenge confronting people or situation that may impact security or harmony.*

Expressive-*like to be the "life of the party," or enjoys being the center of attention; they like to express themselves in the way they dress, the things they own, etc. They will do almost anything to get and keep themselves in the spotlight. They are very creative, spontaneous and fun filled people. People focused rather than task focused.*

Exercise#4: Answer the following question

What academic subjects (knowledge) do you like or love to learn or can teach other about?

_____

_____

_____

Exercise#5: Answer the following question

What are the things, stuff, events, activities you are passionate about?

_____

_____

_____

#GROUP PRAYER

End your study session with a prayer based on the skills and principles taught from the lesson.

#PERSONAL CHALLENGE

During the upcoming week complete the following personal profile below.

Name:_____

Age:_____

School/Grade:_____

Church:_____

Parents/Guardian:_____

Favorite Food (Dish):_____

Future Career: _____

What does God's think or say about Me:

_____

_____

_____

My Talents/Skills are:

_____

_____

My Personality Styles are:

_____

"For I know the plans I have for you," says the LORD . "They are plans for good and not for disaster, to give you a future and a hope." (Jeremiah 29:11 NLT)

LESSON #3

THE TEAM

THE TEAM

"The quality of your life is determined by the quality of your relationships."
-Cedric J. Beckles.

INTRODUCTION

In car racing, the driver's goal is to win the championship trophy. The Team Leader sets the plan to achieve that purpose. The driver executes the program, and the team members play supporting roles in the execution of the plan. The support functions include people working both in front and behind the scene ensuring that the driver prepares for the race, competes in the race, finishes the race and has the best possible performance in the race. Some of the team members in car racing are Engine Specialist, Tire Specialist, Engineers, General Mechanics, Pit Crew, Truck Driver, Administrative personnel and Marketing personnel.

Just as in car racing, to be successful during your life's race, you will need people, systems, and tools to help you. God, the Team Leader, will connect you (the driver) with the right people at different stages of your race. These people will be the path or tool to shape, sharpen, prune, redirect, develop and grow you. They will also assist in helping you to identify and develop your skills, experiences, talents, personality styles, passions, and knowledge.

The driver cannot win the championship trophy without a Team Leader or a team. Now let's look at your path to your championship trophy and examine the roles and responsibilities of specific types of people you will need for your life's race:

- Parents
- Coaches/ Mentors
- Teachers
- Counselor/Advisors
- Leaders (*Church, Government, School, and Community*)
- Friends

#CHECK THIS OUT!

"As iron sharpens iron, so a friend sharpens a friend." (Proverbs 27:17 NLT)

#PRESS PLAY

Watch the Video or PowerPoint Lesson on **The Team.** Follow and fill in the blanks in your workbook. Feel free to jot down any points, quotes, or ideas that have impacted you.

PARENTS

1. These are the most _____persons in your life.

2. They provide _____, _____, _____, and _____ during your life's race.

3. They act as _____, _____, _____, _____, _____, _____and _____during your life's race.

COACHES/MENTORS

1. A coach or mentor is a person who forms a _____relationship with you.

2. A coach or mentor helps you _____ and _____ your potential in particular skill, talent, behavior, knowledge, personality, passion, and practices.

3. A coach or mentor helps you to narrow your _____ and helps you _____.

4. Coaches and mentors are able to extract _____ and _____ out of you.

Great Sports Coaches/Mentors

- *Phil Jackson*

  o *He is considered one of the best coaches in the history of the National Basketball Association (NBA). He identified, enhanced and developed the skills of two of the greatest NBA players and helped them become iconic; Kobe Byrant and Michael Jordan. Through his coaching of these great players; Kobe Byrant won 5 NBA championships, and Michael Jordan won 6 NBA championships.*

- *Vince Lombardi (Green Bay Packers)*

  o *The National Football League (NFL) championship trophy is named after him. He was able to motivate, teach and inspire his team to become the most dominating NFL team of the 1960s.*

Great Biblical Coaches/Mentors

- *Apostle Paul*

  o *He met Timothy who was a young man, and he coached/mentored him, helping him develop his potential. Timothy became a missionary, evangelist, and administrator. Apostle Paul is believed to have written 13 of the 27 books of the New Testament.*

- *Jesus Christ*

  o *He is considered the greatest mentor and teacher in history, he selected disciples (mentees), who left their jobs and followed him.*
  o *Jesus spent about three years with his disciples and modeled love, patience, friendship, leadership, discipleship, handling challenges, generosity, and kindness.*
  o *Jesus' disciples (mentees) in turn taught many others and developed Christianity into a worldwide religion.*

TEACHERS

1. A teacher is a person who imparts _____.

2. A teacher will help you _____ by providing you with learning lessons.

3. The teacher is focused on your _____, recognition and _____ of facts and knowledge.

4. A good teacher will possess the necessary _____, _____, _____, and _____ for teaching.

Biblical Teachers:

*   *Paul and Barnabas were teachers, they taught the new believers at Antioch. Paul also taught at other places like Corinth and Ephesus.*

    "So Paul stayed there for the next year and a half, teaching the word of God." (Acts 18:11 NLT)

COUNSELORS/ADVISORS

1. A counselor is a person who will form a relationship with you to _____ you through a period of hurt or _____ (mentally or emotionally).

2. A counselor or advisor will help you _____ your pain, loss, hurt and emotional wounds.

3. A counselor or advisor will also assist you with handling _____, disappointments, _____ and _____.

Biblical Counselors:

There are many examples of counseling being carried out in the Bible: Jesus Christ was a counselor. Nathan also counseled David.

"Then David confessed to Nathan, "I have sinned against the LORD." Nathan replied, "Yes, but the LORD has forgiven you, and you won't die for this sin." (2 Samuel 12:13 NLT)

LEADERS

1. A leader is a person who has _____ and _____ over a group of followers.

2. Leaders are found in all areas of your life, _____, _____, _____, _____, etc.

3. The ultimate leader in your life is _____.

4. The Bible instructs us to _____, _____ and _____ our leaders appropriately.

5. Your success in your life's race is connected to your _____ to the leaders in your life.

Biblical Leaders:

*   There are numerous examples of leaders in the Bible: Abraham, Moses, Joshua, Saul, David, Solomon, Elijah, Elisha, Esther, Deborah, Jesus, Paul, and Peter.

    "Instead, commission Joshua and encourage and strengthen him, for he will lead the people across the Jordan. He will give them all the land you now see before you as their possession." (Deuteronomy 3:28 NLT)

FRIENDS

God designed you as a social being. You were meant to connect, share and communicate appropriately with other people. You were designed to have fellowship, intimacy, and closeness with family, friends, etc.

1. God (Team Leader) desires an _____ with you.

2. He sent His Son, Jesus Christ, to _____ the connection that was lost in the Garden of Eden.

    "When the cool evening breezes were blowing, the man and his wife heard the LORD God walking about in the garden. So they hid from the LORD God among the trees" (Genesis 3:8 NLT)

3. Not connecting appropriately with others leads to _____, _____, _____, etc.

It is important to select the right type of friends because of the importance and impact that friendship has on your life.

When you choose your friends, ensure they have the following ten Biblical characteristics:

1. Friends _____ you. (*Proverbs 17:9*)

2. Friends love _____. (*Proverbs 17:17*)

3. Friends are _____. (*Proverbs 18:24*)

4. Friends speak the _____ at the _____ and in the _____. (*Proverbs 24:26*)

5. Friends _____ you. (*Proverbs 27:17*)

6. Friends _____ you. (*Proverbs 25:9-10*)

7. Friends _____ with open, honest, real words with a level of care. (*John 14:15*)

8. Friends give sound _____. (*Proverbs 27:9*)

9. Friends speak the _____ in love. (*Proverbs 27:6*)

10. Friends _____ you. (*Job 6:14*)

Biblical Friends:

- David and Jonathan

  o King Saul wanted to kill David because he was jealous of him. However, Jonathan, son of King Saul understanding his father's intention intervened and save David's life (*1 Samuel 20:1-42*).

  o David eventually became King of Israel and despite how he was treated, restored King Saul's possession to Jonathan's disabled son, Mephibosheth.

#GROUP CHAT

Take 10-15 minutes to answer the questions below in your workbook and then discuss your answers with your group:

Exercise#1: Answer the following question

Name 2 persons in your life who acts a coach/mentor and identify what qualities or potential are they trying to develop in you.

1._____

2._____

Name 1-2 persons in your life who acts a teacher and what knowledge did they give you.

1._____

    2._____

Name 1-2 persons in your life who acts a counselor/advisor. How did they helped you to heal emotionally or mentally.

1._____

    2._____

Name 1-2 persons in your life who are leaders and what areas of your life are they leading you?

1._____

    2._____

Exercise#2: Name 3 persons in your life who are friends and list two Biblical characteristics each possess from the list above.

1. Name:_____

    a. Biblical Characteristic:_____

2. Name:_____

3. Biblical Characteristic_____

4. Name:_____

    a. Biblical Characteristic:_____

#GROUP PRAYER

End your study session with a prayer based on the skills and principles taught from the lesson.

#PERSONAL CHALLENGE

During the upcoming week complete the following challenge by reading the information below and then answering the associated questions:

Are you an Eagle or a Chicken?

Remember you are influenced and impacted by the people you connect with. Your friendships and relationships determine whether you are a chicken or an eagle.

God identified Himself with two animals in the Bible, the eagle, and the lion. Both animals are the kings in their dominion.

Let's look at the eagle (king of the birds) and compare it with another bird (the chicken) to learn how leaders think and behave.

Eagles:

- Live in the sky and see the big picture.
- Travel alone, are responsible and are leaders.
- Patient and waits for the right moment to soar.
- Provider, trainer, and protector for his family.
- Focuses on what it needs to do without concern for what others are doing.
- Faces an approaching storm and uses it to soar and glide higher.
- Risk takers.

The eagle's behavior makes them successful.

Chickens:

- Spend their life on the ground, they see life from a small perspective.
- Hang with a crowd, they are followers.
- Lives in the same conditions for their entire life. They have a low desire to grow and develop.
- Hang out in the yard fighting and squabbling.
- Only want stuff when someone else wants it.
- Sees the approaching storm and becomes afraid, panics and seeks shelter.
- They are not risk takers.

Do you behave like the eagle or the chicken?

_____

Would you describe your friends as eagles or chickens?

_____

What do you need to change in your life to behave more like an eagle?

_____

"But those who trust in the LORD will find new strength. They will soar high on wings like eagles. They will run and not grow weary. They will walk and not faint.." (Isaiah 40:31 NLT)

LESSON #4

MONEY

MONEY

"I believe that through knowledge and discipline, financial peace is possible for all of us."
- Dave Ramsey

INTRODUCTION

Money is the tool or resource that will be used to fund your life's activities, vision, goals, and events. It is critical that you learn about the management of money for your life's race. How you manage money significantly impacts how well you navigate, enjoy and end your life's race.

Car racing teams and their drivers gain money (income) from racing, endorsements, and licensing revenue. This revenue is used for the activities of the team which can include the design and maintenance of the car, team, and driver. The Team Leader, team, and driver, must manage the financial resources well to ensure there is funds for salaries, pay vendors, purchase tools and needed resources, transport equipment and people where needed, etc. Poor management of money will significantly impact the efficient operations of the team.

In your life's race, you can potentially earn money from different sources; but it's more important that you learn how to be a good money manager. This is one of the critical areas in your life that you must learn and master. If you don't manage money, you will not be able to fund goals and activities during your life's race. Additionally, poor money management leads to stress, health and relational issues.

In this lesson, we will learn about the principles of stewardship (money manager), budgeting, giving, savings and investments, debt, utilizing insurance and potential online business applications.

#CHECK THIS OUT!

"The master was full of praise. 'Well done, my good and faithful servant. You have been faithful in handling this small amount, so now I will give you many more responsibilities. Let's celebrate together!'" (Matthew 25:2 NLT)

#PRESS PLAY

Watch the Video or PowerPoint Lesson on **Money.** Follow and fill in the blanks in your workbook. Feel free to jot down any points, quotes, or ideas that have impacted you.

STEWARDSHIP 101

1. The word of God advises us to handle our money and material resources based on the principle of _____.

2. All of your _____and _____ were given and is owned by God.

3. You are responsible for _____ of your possessions (*time, money, talents, skills, knowledge, relationships, level of influence, etc.*) according to God's will and desires.

4. To be a wise steward (manager, administrator), learn and follow _____.

"The earth is the LORD 's, and everything in it. The world and all its people belong to him." (Psalms 24:1 NLT)

SPENDING PLAN/BUDGET

1. One of the most effective ways to manage or administer money is by using a
   _____ _____.

2. Money comes from _____ (*income, allowance, business, etc.*).

3. A spending plan is a _____ of how you will spend the money that you
   will be entrusted with.

4. In this plan you will list your _____ along with all expenses (*household,
   utilities, debt, education, recreation, insurance, health, etc.*).

5. The spending plan should always end in _____ (every cent should be
   accounted for).

6. To make your spending plan work, you will need to track your _____
   daily.

Tip-Buying Groceries

- *Offer to help your parents with the grocery shopping*
- *Make a shopping list*
- *Stay focused on your shopping list*
- *Set a spending limit*
- *Stay within your spending limit*

GIVING

1. God desires for us to give of the _____ that he blesses us with and wants
   us to be _____ givers (*2 Corinthians 9:7*).

2. We should also have a _____ and _____ attitude to help
   the poor. (Proverbs 19:17)

3. A portion of your income should be given to your _____ to support the
   work of God's on earth. (*1 Corinthians 9:14*)

4. We can honor _____ by giving the first portion of our income to him.
   (*Proverbs 3:9*)

5. Giving means more than donating _____, we can give off our _____, _____ and other material resources (*serving in a church, library, nursing home, donating clothes, shoes, books, etc.*).

Tip-Managing a Home

Expenses for a home:

- o *Mortgage or Rental fees*
- o *Yard Maintenance*
- o *Taxes*
- o *Utilities (Electricity, water, cable, the internet)*
- o *Insurance*

SAVING & INVESTMENTS

1. There are many ways you can _____ or _____.

2. Remember to setup an automatic savings deduction of _____ of your income, this should be done before paying your expenses.

3. _____ is charged on money that is put into a saving account, this a way to gain additional money or invest.

4. A saving account along with investment options is beneficial for _____, _____ and _____ _____ (*education, cell phone, vacation, electronics, clothing*).

5. There are many _____ and _____ options, they differ based on the returns and the levels of risk:

   a. _____

   b. _____

   c. _____

   d. _____

   e. _____

   f. _____

Tip-Money for Vacation or Shopping Trip

- *Use a spending plan*
- *Use a shopping list*
- *Look for sales and off season items*
- *Keep your focus on your shopping list*
- *Expenses include:*
    - *Hotel*
    - *Car and gas*
    - *Food and snacks*
    - *Entertainment*
    - *Shopping expenses*
    - *Travel Tickets*

This will help you understand how much money your parent need for your family shopping and vacation trips

COMPOUND INTEREST

1. Compound interest is the _____ that is calculated on the initial amount of money and the accumulated interest.

2. The earlier you start using _____, the more money you can earn.

Age	Investment	Total Value
19	$2000	$2,200
20	$2000	$4,620
21	$2000	$7,282
22	$2000	$10,210
23	$2000	$13,431
24	$2000	$16,974
25	$2000	$20,871
26*	$2000	$25,158
35	$0	$59,322
47	$0	$188,180
65	$0	**$1,035,148**

*The investment amount after age 26 becomes $0 annually up to the age of 65yrs, the annual return is 10%.
(Source: The Time Value of Money, The Finish Rich Workbook by David Bach)*

RETIREMENT

1. This is an investment tool used to save money for your _____.

2. The best time to open a retirement account is when you are a _____.

3. The later you start _____ the more difficult it is to catch up.

4. Using _____ you can save over $1,000, 000 when you reach age 65 (*starting at age 19*).

DEBT

1. Debt makes you a _____ to whom you owe money.

2. There are cases where going into debt may be necessary; however, the money you borrow should be handled _____ and ensure that the debt is _____.

3. When you borrow money (*loans etc.*), it must be repaid within a _____. (*Proverbs 37:21*)

4. _____ is charged on loans.

5. There are different types of debt such as _____, _____, _____ and line of credit.

6. Be careful of _____, they tend to encourage spending which can lead to unnecessary debt.

7. Credit cards should be used _____, where possible use a _____ which only allows you to spend what is deposited in the account.

Credit Card Debt Exercise:

A typical credit card balance of $5,600 with an 18% interest rate, making the minimum payment of $100 a month, will take _____ years to pay off providing that no other charges are made to the card.

However, if an extra _____ is paid per month, it will take _____ years to pay off the balance and the interest would have amounted to $1,640. This is a saving of approx. _____ and two years of payments!
Whenever you shop with a credit card, you are paying an additional 18% on your purchases

"Just as the rich rule the poor, so the borrower is servant to the lender." (Proverbs 22:7 NLT)

INSURANCE

1. Insurance is a way to protect against _____.

2. The insurance company makes a _____ to compensate in the event of a loss.

3. The insurance company charges a fee called a _____.

4. The customer is known as the _____ and receives a contract for payments (*insurance policy*).

5. When there is a loss, a _____ is submitted to the insurance company by the policyholder (*insured*).

6. The insurance company _____ the money so that it can gain additional money (interest) for payment of claims and operational expenses for the insurance.

7. There are different types of _____ (auto, life, medical, disability, rental, etc).

Tip-Cost of College/University Education

- *Getting a College or University education is very expensive. The cost and expenses include:*

  o *Tuition (cost for teaching sessions)*
  o *Services Fees (library, parking, student activities)*
  o *Housing (room and board)*
  o *Books & School supplies*
  o *Personal expenses(transportation, trips, etc.)*

  (Collegedata.com reports that in the USA the moderate annual cost for an in-state public college is $24,610 and for a private college is $49,320 -2016/2017)

ONLINE BUSINESS

1. The Internet and technology based tools are not just for _____ (*Facebook, Twitter, Instagram, etc.*), _____ and games.

2. These are also powerful tools that can be used to assist in your _____ and development or to help you in creating a successful _____.

3. Here are some ways you can earn a wholesome income online:

- Doing a _____.

- Subscription _____ services.

- As a _____.

- Writing _____.

- Online _____.

- _____ items.

- _____.

- _____ services.

- Market research for _____.

- _____ stuff.

#GROUP CHAT

Take 10-15 minutes to answer the questions below in your workbook and then discuss your answers with your group:

Exercise#1: If you were held accountable for how well you are managing your time, money, talents, skills, knowledge, relationships, the level of influence, what grade would you receive?

A ☐

B ☐

C ☐

D ☐

E ☐

F ☐

Exercise#2: Review the monthly budget below for a teenager and answer the following questions

Description	Date	Earn	Spend
Got money from parents	July 3	$15	
Went to movies	July 5		$15
Purchase minutes for cell phone	July 9		$10
Wash the car	July 12	$10	
Run errand for Mommy	July 15	$15	
Purchase burger and fries with soda	July 18		$7
Went out with friends	July 21		$20
Total	n/a	$40	$52

Compare the income of the teenager versus their total expenses, what did you notice?

_____

_____

_____

_____

What actions would you suggest this teenager do to cut expenses?

_____

_____

_____

_____

Exercise#3: Pretend you needed to save $500 for a want such as a video game, cell phone, clothes, shoes or a trip, create a savings goal plan to achieve this target. See a savings goal plan diagram below.

SMART goal: Save $500 by December 31st.

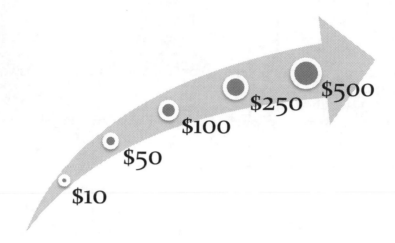

What will you use the $500 for?

_____

_____

Where will you get the money from?

_____

_____

How often will you save money?

_____

_____

Where will you store the money?

_____

_____

#PERSONAL CHALLENGE

Exercise#1: Complete the table below about different types of investments:

Types of Investments	Definition	Returns	Risk
Stock	Percentage of ownership in a publicly held company		High Risk
Bonds			Low Risk
Mutual Funds	Shares in a collection of stocks/bonds or securities purchased as one package		Medium Risk
Fixed Deposit			
Annuity	Retirement Investment issued by an insurance company		

Exercise#2: During the week, plan a party for you and your friends at your home. Plan a meal and activities (what will it include), determine how much the items will cost and ways that you can keep the cost down. Compare the cost for the party at home versus you and your friends going out to a restaurant.

MONEY TERMS

Account Statement-a record of transactions in an account in a bank or an investment firm or company.

Allowance- a small amount of money that a parent or guardian gives to a child/teenage etc.

Bond- when the government or company promises to repay money that was borrowed from investors at a specific time and pay interest at a specific rate.

Budget- a spending plan based on your income and expenses.

Compound Interest- this is interest that is paid on the principal and on the interest that has been earned.

Credit- when you borrow money or charge your items to an account before you paid for the items.

Debit Card- a card that allows you to do transactions by transferring your money electronically from your account to the retailer.

Debt- money that you borrow, that must be repaid with interest at a specified time.

Deposit- the money that is in an account whether it is in a bank, trust company or a credit union.

Discretionary income- what remains from your income after you paid for all your essential expenses (such as food, clothing, household expenses).

Expenses- money used for item or service to a person or a group of people.

Income- money you received from wages, salaries, profit, interest payments, rent or other types of earnings.

Interest- a fee that is paid either to borrow or save money.

Investing- when money is used to gain financially, with an expectation that it will provide a return.

Loan – money borrowed for a particular period of time with an agreed rate of interest.

Mutual Fund- money invested along with a group of investors managed by a money manager.

Need- something that is a necessity or that is essential.

Payroll Deductions- when money is automatically deducted from your income for taxes, job-related deductions (insurance, pension contributions) etc.

Principal- money that was initially save, invested or borrowed that will earn interest.

Return-profit made from an investment.

Risk- the level of uncertainty regarding a return from an investment.

Savings- money that is put aside in an account for immediate or future needs. Interest is also gain on savings.

Simple interest- interest that is paid only on your initial investment or deposit earned over a period of time.

Stock-ownership in a company

Want- something that is desired and is not a necessity.

LESSON#5

PITSTOPS

PIT STOPS

"Rest when you're weary. Refresh and renew yourself, your body, your mind, your spirit. Then get back to work."
-Ralph Marston

INTRODUCTION

In car racing, the role of the driver is to navigate the car around the race track, from the start to the finish line. The race conditions are not always ideal. There may be weather changes, crashes or unexpected behaviors of the other drivers. To successfully navigate the race track, both the car and driver must take pit stops. These are short periods when the pit stop team members must refuel, make minor repairs and change the tires of the car. The pit stop is also a rest stop for the driver. During the pit stop, while the car is in neutral, the driver rests and keeps his feet on the brakes. Car racing is one of the most demanding sports which require a high level of concentration, discipline, and stamina. Due to these demands, the driver must take good care of his or her physical body and soul (*thoughts, ambitions, feelings, and conscience*). The timing of the pit stops is planned and designed by the Team Leader. A successful racing team is skilled at having efficient pit stops.

You are the driver of your life's race with the leadership of your Team Leader and support of your team. Your life's race will require discipline, focus, concentration, and stamina. Additionally, there will be challenges, resistance and unexpected conditions during the race. You will need a healthy body and soul to manage these conditions and successfully complete your race. You can maintain your body through proper diet, exercise, sleep and rest. To keep both your body and soul (*thoughts, ambitions, feelings, and conscience*), you will need to take periodic breaks or pit stops. These periods of pause will help you re-focus, communicate with the Team Leader and critical team members, make adjustments, repair and replenish yourself. This, also provides a rest point to review your current state, life conditions and future targets. After each pit stop, you should be re-energized and refreshed to resume your race and face whatever challenge you encounter.

In this lesson, we will learn about the activities you will need to complete during your pit stops for a healthy body and soul during your life's race.

#CHECK THIS OUT!

"Guard your heart above all else, for it determines the course of your life." (Proverbs 4:23 NLT)

#PRESS PLAY

Watch the Video or PowerPoint Lesson on *Pit Stops.* Follow and fill in the blanks in your workbook. Feel free to jot down any points, quotes, or ideas that have impacted you.

THE PIT STOP

In car racing, there are pit stops during the race. These pit stops are necessary for the maintenance of both the car and the driver.

1. The Pit Stop is _____, where minor repairs, tire changes along with refueling are done to the driver's car.

2. During a pit stop, while the car is being _____the driver sits in _____and keeps his foot on the _____.

3. The Pit Stop is _____ to the success of the driver during the race.

4. You will need to take _____ from your activities just like a car needs to make pit stops.

5. Our pit stops should consist of _____, biblical meditation, _____, sleep, _____, and reflection.

6. Your life's race without _____will lead to problems just like a race car that does not take breaks to refuel, complete minor repairs and change its tires.

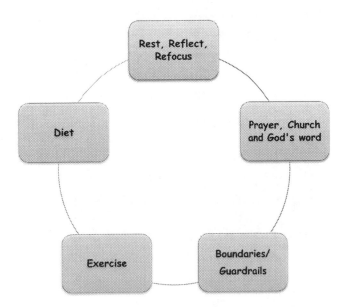

REST, REFLECT AND RE-FOCUS

1. Sleep is the body's natural _____.

2. When you get adequate sleep:

   a. You will be _____ and _____.

   b. You will be alert to _____.

   c. You will be _____ emotionally.

   d. You will reduce _____ in your brain.

3. Shawn Stevenson in his book "*Sleep Smarter*" states that not having enough sleep leads to _____, _____, _____, cancer, _____ and issues with your immune system.

4. According to research, teenagers need about _____ hours of sleep daily (*www.nationwidechildrens.org/sleep-in-adolescents*).

PRAYER, THE BIBLE, AND CHURCH

1. _____ is a pit stop when you pause from your activities to talk with God.

2. It is talking to _____ as you would when talking to a friend.

3. When you chat with God, you can share _____, _____, _____ mistakes, failures, _____ and _____ etc.

4. Reading God's word (the Bible) is a pit stop where you gain _____ from the Team Leader regarding your _____ and _____ during your life's race.

5. Attending church is a pit stop where you _____, encourage, _____ and _____ with other Christians.

"And let us not neglect our meeting together, as some people do, but encourage one another, especially now that the day of his return is drawing near." (Hebrews 10:25 NLT)

BOUNDARIES/GUARDRAILS

1. _____ are essential for good health, they are necessary for your activities, your decisions, your relationships, etc.

2. Boundaries let people know _____and are associated with pit stops.

3. There are usually _____ whenever your boundaries are crossed.

4. Saying _____is a pit stop and is a means of implementing boundaries or limits.

5. Setting up _____ in our life will keep us from dangerous and tragic consequences.

ACCIDENT, CURVES, BAD WEATHER

1. There will be _____, resistance, and _____ conditions during your life's race.

2. You will need to take a pit stop to _____, recommit, _____with the Team Leader (God) and pray during these periods of your journey.

3. You will need to refocus on _____, his _____ for your life, your _____ and action steps.

4. Decide that you will never _____.

5. When you fail or make mistakes during your life's race, _____ from them and then _____your run.

DIET

1. To maintain good health, you should eat a _____,_____ diet.

2. You should think that what you _____ and _____really impacts your health

3. A balanced diet will have the right amount of _____, fats, _____, vitamins, _____, and water that are needed for good health.

EXERCISE

1. Being _____ is essential to your health.

2. Use an instrument like _____ to track your daily movement.

3. Based on research teenagers should get at least _____ of exercise daily to burns calories. (*http://kidshealth.org/en/parents/fitness-13-18.html*)

4. Exercise helps to eliminate _____ from your system, and it improves your _____.

5. Exercise also helps with your _____.

#GROUP CHAT

Take 10-15 minutes to answer the questions below in your workbook and then discuss your answers with your group:

Exercise#1: Answer the following questions about your diet:

What are your typical lunch, weekday and Sunday meals?

_____

_____

_____

_____

_____

_____

_____

_____

Would you consider these meals healthy or unhealthy?

_____

_____

If your answer to the above question is unhealthy, what do you need to changes with your to make them healthy?

_____

_____

Exercise#2 Answer the following question related to sleep and exercise:

How many hours of sleep do actually get, is it within the recommended 9 to 9.5hrs daily for teenagers. What do you think is impacting your sleep?

_____

_____

_____

_____

Do you exercise or are involved in any sporting activity at your school, community or church etc?

Yes ☐

No ☐

List below the types of sporting activity you are engage in and how often?

_____

_____

_____

Exercise#3 Answer the following question related to pit stops and boundaries/guardrails:

Do you take regular pit stops (*time to relax, re-focus, reflect and refresh yourself*), if not why not?

_____

_____

_____

What types of boundaries or guardrails do you have? Are these sufficient or do you need more?

_____

_____

_____

_____

_____

_____

#GROUP PRAYER

End your study session with a prayer based on the skills and principles taught from the lesson.

#PERSONAL CHALLENGE

During the upcoming week complete the following challenge by filling out the tracking table below:

- Amount of sleep (*hrs*)
- Meals-breakfast, Lunch, snack, and dinner
- Water intake* (*research the recommended daily intake of water*)
- Recreation Activities

	Monday	Tuesday	Wednesday	Thursday	Friday	Saturday	Sunday
Sleep (hrs)							
Meals							

Water Intake							
Pit Stops							

LESSON #6

RULES & AUTHORITIES

RULES & AUTHORITIES

"... laws [are] not meant to destroy us. But our disobedience leads to our own destruction."
— Lailah Gifty Akita

INTRODUCTION

In car racing, there are rules that apply to every aspect of the sport. There are rules that relate to the drivers' conduct, the number of cars in the race, the design and building of the race car, the display on the car, the way to overtake, and the pit stops. All teams and drivers have to govern themselves according to these rules and regulations. The racing authorities are responsible for making and enforcing these laws. Similarly, for your life's race, there are rules by which you must be governed. In our society, there are also authorities who are responsible for making and enforcing the law or rules. This will ensure that we live and thrive in a civil society.

God requires us to honor the authorities and the laws (rules) within the society in which we live (*Romans 13:1*). Therefore, it is important that we know and understand where laws come from, the different levels of authority, and why it is important to be subjected to those laws.

In this lesson, we will learn about where laws came from, why it is important to follow the rules and the different levels of authority *(home, church, state, & individual)* that should govern your life's race.

#CHECK THIS OUT!

"In those days Israel had no king; everyone did as they saw fit." (Judges 21:25 NLT)

#PRESS PLAY

Watch the Video or PowerPoint Lesson on **Rules & Authorities.** Follow and fill in the blanks in your workbook. Feel free to jot down any points, quotes, or ideas that have impacted you.

WHERE LAWS COME FROM?

1. Laws were provided by _____.

2. God gave His people the _____ along with other rules.

3. Subsequently, ancient societies _____ these laws (*including the Romans*), and eventually, they were entrenched in the laws of modern societies.

WHY DO I NEED TO FOLLOW THEM?

1. Laws were given by God to provide _____ and to _____ them.

2. These laws were given to teach the people:

   • The right way to treat _____.

   • The right way to treat _____.

   • The right way to treat _____.

Therefore, it is important that we follow them.

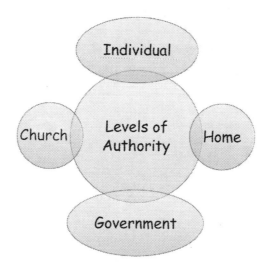

Interesting Facts about the Bible

- *There are 66 books in the Bible.*
- *The Old Testament has 39 books.*
- *The Old Testament was originally written in Hebrew.*
- *The New Testament has 27 books .*
- *The New Testament was originally written in Greek.*

- *The Bible is the world's most shoplifted book even though you can get it for free!*
- *The Bible has more sold copies than any other book in history, it is the world's best-selling and most widely distributed book.*
- *The Bible has over 40 authors.*

Source: www.biblereasons.com/bible-facts/

THE HOME

1. The home was established by God (*Genesis 1:28*), firstly consisting of the _____and then the children.

2. There was an order of _____in the home.

3. The home is to be an example, provide an example, teach _____ & _____, nurture identity, and provide _____ (*basic needs of humans*).

4. The Bible tells us that the responsibility of the children is to _____ and _____their parents. (*Ephesians 6:1-2*)

5. The Bible says that the responsibilities of the parents are to _____and _____their children, but they should not provoke them. (*Psalms 22:6, Ephesians 6:4*)

   "God blessed them and said to them, "Be fruitful and increase in number; fill the earth and subdue it. Rule over the fish in the sea and the birds in the sky and over every living creature that moves on the ground." (Genesis 1:28 NLT)

THE GOVERNMENT

1. The government is a level of authority that was established by _____. (*Romans 13:4*)

2. The function of government is to:

   a. _____.

   b. provide _____.

   c. provide _____.

    d. act on behalf of the _____ of all its people.

    e. create the conditions for an _____ and _____ society.

3. The Bible teaches us to _____, honor and _____ for our government leaders. (*1 Timothy 2:2*)

4. We are also taught by God _____ the laws and be _____ to government.

"Let everyone be subject to the governing authorities, for there is no authority except that which God has established. The authorities that exist have been established by God." (Romans 13:1 NLT)

LEGAL AUTHORITIES-GOVERNMENT

THE POLICE

1. The roles of the Police in society are to:

    a. Observe potential _____.

    b. _____ criminal and civil activities.

    c. Conduct _____.

    d. Respond to _____.

    e. Issue traffic-related _____.

    f. Make _____.

    g. _____ when needed in legal proceedings.

LAWYERS & JUDGES

1. Lawyers also use their _____ to solve legal problems.

2. Judges are legal authorities that should be _____.

3. They are also responsible for:

    a. _____ the law,

    b. _____the evidence that is presented

    c. _____ hearings and trials in their courtrooms.

4. Once the legal proceeding is completed, a _____ is given by the judge followed by either a sentencing or a fine.

THE CHURCH

1. The church is a level of authority that was established by _____.

2. The church is a body of _____who are called and saved through the process of repentance and faith in Jesus Christ.

3. The work of the church also includes _____ those who are not Christians (lost or unsaved).

4. The church consists of members with _____ that were given by God.

5. These members are to use their gifts to edify, _____, build and _____ the body of believers.

6. The church provides a forum for public worship, _____, spiritual disciplines, _____, discipleship and _____for its members.

THE INDIVIDUAL

1. The individual is another level of authority established by _____.

2. The person governs himself/herself based on God and his word, this is _____ _____.

3. Personal responsibility means that you are willing to _____ and _____by the standards that the society established for the behavior of its citizens.

4. You must learn to take _____in all areas of your life's race (e.g. *use of your talents and abilities, management of money, your body, your education, your sexual behavior, career/job, marriage and friends*) or else you will suffer the consequences.

5. When there are _____, you must not _____ others or something else but be accountable for your actions.

"Now all has been heard; here is the conclusion of the matter: Fear God and keep his commandments, for this is the duty of all mankind. For God will bring every deed into judgment, including every hidden thing, whether it is good or evil." (Ecclesiastes 12:13-14 NLT)

THE INDIVIDUAL (BEHAVIOR)

CHARACTER

1. Your character is who you _____ , it's how you behave even when no one is _____.

2. Your character determines your _____ regardless of the circumstances and challenges during your life's race.

3. Good character involves having and displaying _____, dependability, _____, humility, _____, and a _____.

VALUES

1. Values are what you believe is _____ (priorities).

2. Your values affect all _____of your life (*where you will live, how you spend money, how you spend your time and energy, your interaction with people, how hard you work, the type of parent you will become, etc.*).

3. Identification of your _____ is essential for your life's race.

Common Values	**Common Values**	**Common Values**
Kindness	Fairness	Security
Loyalty	Intelligence	Happiness
Beauty	Adventure	Peace of mind
Community	Power/Authority	Fun
Education	Family	Friends
Honesty	Confidence/Boldness	Marriage
Generosity	Fulfillment	Making a difference
Love	Independence	Growth
Health		Creativity

DISCIPLINE/SELF-CONTROL

1. This is the ability to _____ your behavior and actions even under difficult or challenging situations.

2. We can manage ourselves through _____, avoidance, _____, boundaries and _____.

YOUR MOUTH AND THOUGHTS

1. Your thinking or thoughts generate your _____, what you _____ ideas and _____ your behavior.

2. To make the changes in your life, you will need to change how you _____. (*Philippians 2:5, Mark 9:23*).

3. God teaches us _____ and what to _____.

4. What you say can determine how you _____ and how _____.

5. Your words also impact how you _____ and _____.

"Finally, brothers and sisters, whatever is true, whatever is noble, whatever is right, whatever is pure, whatever is lovely, whatever is admirable—if anything is excellent or praiseworthy—think about such things." (Philippians 4:8 NLT)

#GROUP CHAT

Take 10-15 minutes to answer the questions below in your workbook and then discuss your answers with your group:

Exercise#1: Answer the following questions.

List 2-3 laws from your country below:

_____

_____

_____

_____

Describe your home (*Father and Mother present, Single parent, No parents but a Guardian, etc*).

_____

Describe the system of government in your country.

_____

_____

_____

List your values below (*using the table of common values above*):

_____

_____

_____

_____

Exercise#2: Complete the following self-assessment:

Rate yourself below on the following character traits

Character Trait	Rating
Humble	1 2 3 4 5
Reliable	1 2 3 4 5
Teachable	1 2 3 4 5
Respectful	1 2 3 4 5
Responsible	1 2 3 4 5
Kind	1 2 3 4 5
Self-discipline	1 2 3 4 5
Polite	1 2 3 4 5
Compassionate	1 2 3 4 5
Honesty	1 2 3 4 5

What was your total score? _____

What are the areas in which you need to work?

_____

_____

Have someone in your group who knows you rate you below on the following character traits

Character Trait	Rating
Humble	1 2 3 4 5
Reliable	1 2 3 4 5
Teachable	1 2 3 4 5
Respectful	1 2 3 4 5
Responsible	1 2 3 4 5
Kind	1 2 3 4 5
Self-discipline	1 2 3 4 5
Polite	1 2 3 4 5
Compassionate	1 2 3 4 5
Honesty	1 2 3 4 5

What was the total score? _____

Exercise#3: Answer the following questions.

Do you take personal responsibility for your decisions, mistakes, actions etc., or do you blame others, make excuses? Describe your behavior below:

_____

_____

_____

_____

Do your friends take personal responsibility for their decisions, mistakes, actions etc., or do they tend to blame others, or make excuses? Describe their behavior below:

_____

_____

_____

_____

#GROUP PRAYER

End your study session with a prayer based on the skills and principles taught from the lesson.

#PERSONAL CHALLENGE

During the upcoming week have your parent(s) rate you and compare all of your scores for your character traits.

Parent(s):

Character Trait	Rating
Humble	1 2 3 4 5
Reliable	1 2 3 4 5
Teachable	1 2 3 4 5
Respectful	1 2 3 4 5
Responsible	1 2 3 4 5
Kind	1 2 3 4 5
Self-discipline	1 2 3 4 5
Polite	1 2 3 4 5
Compassionate	1 2 3 4 5
Honesty	1 2 3 4 5

What was the total score from your parent? _____

When you compare all of your scores, were they similar or different?

_____

_____

_____

LESSON #7

RACE RESOURCES

RACE RESOURCES

*"Our life is the sum total of all the decisions we make every day,
and those decisions are determined by our priorities."*
-Myles Munroe

INTRODUCTION

To be fully prepared for a race, the race car driver must have several resources. These resources are the car, gloves, fire protective suits, helmet, head and neck support system, seat belt and shoes. These resources play several different roles: the gloves, fire protective suits, helmet, head and neck support system, seat belt and shoes are protective tools for the driver himself. While the car is used to start, navigate the racing track and complete the race. It is also designed to protect the driver.

As the driver for your life's race, you too will need several resources. These consists of vision, goals, action steps, education & training, time management skills, employability skills and job readiness skills. You must learn to use and develop these resources or tools to have a successful life's race. These can be categorized as personal and professional development tools. In Lesson# 1 you would have selected a Team Leader and developed some goals for your life's race with the assistance of the Team Leader. In this lesson, we will use that plan to develop goals and an action plan for your life's race.

The focus of the lesson is to identify the resources that you will need for your life's race and then learn how to use them to optimize your winning potential.

#CHECK THIS OUT!

"As the time approached for him to be taken up to heaven, Jesus resolutely set out for Jerusalem." (Luke 9:51 NLT)

#PRESS PLAY

Watch the Video or PowerPoint Lesson on *Racing Resources.* Follow and fill in the blanks in your workbook. Feel free to jot down any points, quotes, or ideas that have impacted you.

Resources

1. Goals
2. Action Steps
3. Time Management
4. Education & Training
5. Job Readiness Skills
6. Employability Skills

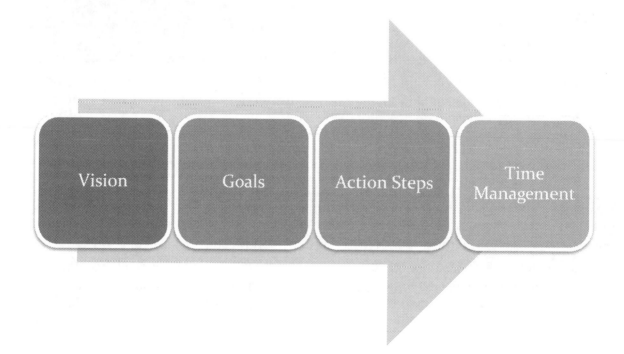

GOALS

1. A _____ is an object that you desire, or are aiming for.

2. Setting goals should be in _____ with the plan God has for our lives.

3. To make your goals useful, you must make them _____ (*a concept introduced in 1981 in the November issue of Management review by George Doran, Arthur Miller, and James Cunningham*).

4. Do not make large _____ of goals.

5. _____ your goals down is a significant step on the road to achieving them. (*Henriette Anne Klauser explains this in her book, Write It Down, Make It Happen: Knowing What You Want And Getting It*)

"We can make our plans, but the Lord determines our steps." (*Proverbs 16:9 NLT*)

Example of SMART Goals

- *Save $500 by August 31st*
- *Purchase a new cell phone by September 30th*
- *Complete a bachelor's degree in Accounting in four (4) years*

6. Your SMART Goals can be divided into _____ periods of your life.

7. Your SMART goals should be _____ periodically

Short Range SMART Goals	Mid Range SMART Goals	Long Range SMART Goals
•_____years	•_____ years	•_____ years

ACTION STEPS

1. For each of your goals, you will need to write out specific _____.

2. Each action step should begin with an _____ word.

3. Each short term goal should have an _____.

4. An immediate action step is an action that can be completed within _____.

5. Action steps should be done daily, _____ or _____ to achieve your goals.

TIME MANAGEMENT

Birth-Infant

Childhood

Adolescent

Young Adult

Adulthood

Late Adulthood

1. Your life has a _____ (birth) and an _____ (death).

2. Your time on the earth is _____ to achieve your goals, vision and the plan God has for your life.

3. Your life also has _____ or _____ like childhood, teenage, young adult, adult, and senior.

4. Each year has _____ months, _____ week and _____ days.

5. Each week there are _____ hours.

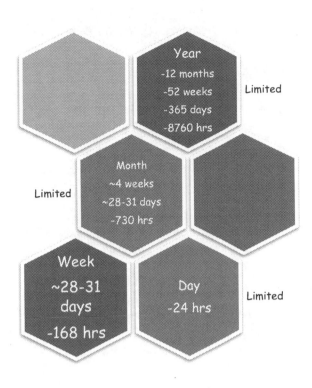

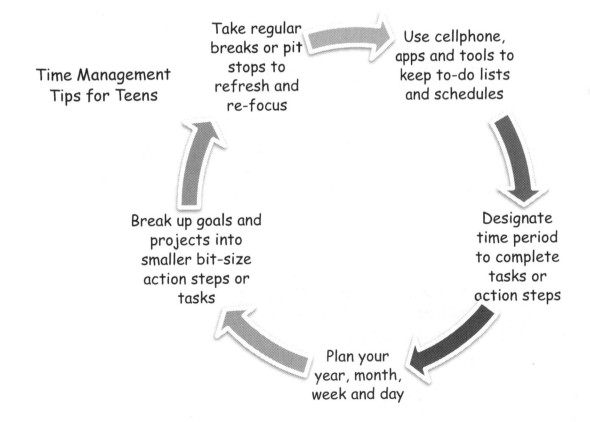

*"To every thing there is a season, and a time to every purpose
under the heaven." (Ecclesiastes 3:1 KJV)*

EDUCATION & TRAINING

1. A quality education will assist you in getting a good job, earn a _____ or income.

2. It will also allow you to _____ in a career or _____ different career options.

3. There are many _____ for getting a good education today due to the advances in technology.

4. You should pursue an education based on a career that you have an _____and _____ for and which is aligned with the purpose God has for your life.

Biblical Education

* Moses grew up in the palace of Egypt as a prince and therefore received the training given to the princes and the royalty of Egypt.
* Moses was able to use that knowledge to administer the civil laws and codes for the nation of Israel while serving as a judge for his people.
* This education given to Moses consisted of science, law and leadership principles. This knowledge and training helped him to handle the challenges of leading his people into the wilderness, to build the tabernacle and write necessary laws and codes.

"At that time Moses was born, and he was no ordinary child. For three months he was cared for by his family. When he was placed outside, Pharaoh's daughter took him and brought him up as her own son." (Acts 7:20-21 NLT)

Types of Academic degrees

* *Associate-typically 2 yrs of study and requires high school completion (diploma/certifications)*
* *Bachelors-typically 4yrs of study and requires high school completion (diploma/certifications)*
* *Masters-typically 1-2 yrs of study and requires Bachelor's degree*
* *Doctoral-typically 2 or more years of study and requires a Masters' degree (some cases may be Bachelor's degree)*

(Source: http://study.com/different_degrees.html)

Types of Technical/Vocational Qualifications

- Short Courses
- Certificate programs
- Diploma programs

Educational or Learning Options

- Online courses
- Webinars
- Seminars
- Workshops
- Podcasts
- Videos

(Source: https://www.personalincome.org/options-education-review/)

JOB READINESS (RESUMES)

1. Make sure it is _____ to read.

2. It should be between _____ pages.

3. Use standard _____ and _____ .

4. Only include _____ related to the job for which you are applying.

5. Use standard _____ .

6. Always tell the _____ .

7. Use a _____ .

8. Use _____ grammar.

9. Do not include a _____ of yourself.

10. Always include your _____ that are relevant to the job you are applying for

11. Highlight _____ skills.

JOB READINESS (INTERVIEWS)

1. Wear _____.

2. Shake the hands of the _____ when entering and leaving the room.

3. Research _____ about the company.

4. Demonstrate appropriate _____skills.

5. Do not make _____ statements about your past employment history.

6. Let the interviewer _____ the meeting.

7. Always wait to be _____.

8. Make _____with the person with whom you are speaking.

9. Know the _____ of your resume.

10. Listen carefully to the questions being asked and _____only to that question.

11. Be _____ in your responses, but show _____ to any requests.

12. Let the interviewer mention _____.

13. Always send a _____for the interview.

EMPLOYABILITY SKILLS

1. These are the necessary skills need for _____, _____ and _____ on a job.

2. These include the _____, _____, and _____ a potential employee will need to interact with his/her potential supervisors and co-workers.

3. These include being able to _____ and _____ appropriately to leadership in the workplace, to make _____ and to demonstrate _____.

4. These are skills that employers want and look for during an _____.

5. Employability skills can be _____.

Essential Employability Skills (needed for any job):

- Communication
- Teamwork.
- Problem-solving.
- Initiative
- Planning Skills
- Basic Time Management and Organizing Skills
- Self-management.
- Learning.
- Use of Technology.

www.youthcentral.vic.gov.au/jobs-careers/planning-your-career/employability-skills

VISION-GOALS-ACTION STEPS

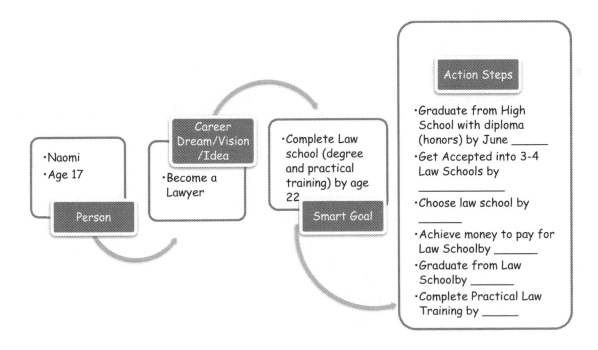

#GROUP CHAT

Take 10-15 minutes to answer the questions below in your workbook and then discuss your answers with your group:

Exercise#1: Identify whether the following goals are SMART:

- Graduate in 3 years with a Law degree _____

- Save $500 within 6 months._____

- Within 5 years, get married and have three children _____

Exercise#2: Use the draft ideas/vision/thoughts that you wrote for the different areas of your life in lesson#1, to write one 1 SMART goal for each area, also identify each SMART goal as short range, middle range or long range:

Health

_____

_____

_____

Job/Career

_____

_____

_____

Relationship with God (Team Leader)

_____

_____

_____

Marriage/Family

_____

_____

_____

Friends

_____

_____

_____

Money

_____

_____

_____

Education or Business

_____

_____

_____

Exercise#3: Using the SMART goals developed above write 2-3 action steps for each SMART goal below. If the SMART goal is a short range goal, it should have an immediate action step as well:

Health

_____

_____

_____

Job/Career

_____

_____

_____

Relationship with God (Team Leader)

_____

_____

_____

Marriage/Family

_____

_____

_____

Friends

_____

_____

_____

Money

_____

_____

_____

Education or Business

_____

_____

_____

#GROUP PRAYER

End your study session with a prayer based on the skills and principles taught from the lesson.

#PERSONAL CHALLENGE

Take some time over the next week to complete the following exercise:

Exercise#1: Answer the following questions related to your future career:

What is your future career choice(s)?

_____

How will you obtain the education needed for your chosen career?

_____

_____

_____

_____

What options for getting a college or earning a tertiary degree/certification/qualification are available in your country?

_____

_____

_____

_____

Write out your current resume below, also explain how your resume would change if you were applying for your future career choice given above. _____

_____

_____

_____

LESSON #8

CONNECT THE PIECES

CONNECT THE PIECES

In this session you will complete an exercise below that incorporates all of the principles and concepts that were taught during the previous seven lessons. Each student (time permitting) should make a brief presentation to the group with their results.

Fill in the blanks below:

1. Name:_____

2. Age:_____

3. School/Grade: _____

4. Church: _____

5. Parents/Guardian: _____

6. Future Career (dream/vision/idea): _____

7. Team Leader (your selection): _____

8. Write out how the Team Leader sees you:

   _____

   _____

   _____

   _____

   _____

9. My skills/talents are:

   _____

   _____

   _____

10. My knowledge/passions are:

_____

_____

_____

11. My personality styles (describe them briefly) are:

_____

_____

_____

12. Write the names of your team members below:

_____

_____

_____

13. Define steward:

_____

_____

_____

14. What is your desired annual salary?_____

15. Using your desired salary listed above, work out the percentage and actual amounts for each budget category below:

Income:	%	Amount
Giving		
Saving		
Household Expenses		
Insurance		
Debt		

Retirement Savings		
Family Expenses (school fee, lunch, clothing, etc.)		
Discretionary		
Misc.		

16. Select (with a check '√' mark) below the following pit stop activities you will use for your life's race:

    a. ◊ Sleep (state desired daily amount):

    b. ◊ Exercise (state desired weekly amount):

    c. ◊ Diet (state desired types of food)

    d. ◊ Spiritual Disciplines (state desired types):

    e. ◊ Recreation-Refresh and Refocus (state desired type, how often)

    f. ◊ Boundaries/Guardrails (state desired ones):

17. List your top three values below:

    _____

    _____

    _____

18. List your top three character traits below:

    _____

    _____

    _____

19. Write one SMART goal for each area of my life below:

Relationship with Team Leader (God)

_____

_____

_____

20. Career/Education/Training

_____

_____

_____

21. Health

_____

_____

_____

22. Money

_____

_____

_____

23. Family/Friend

_____

_____

_____

24. Ministry (Service)

_____

_____

_____

25. Label each SMART goal above as either short, mid or long range goals:

26. Take each short range goal and create 2-3 action steps each, also write out the time period when you will complete the action step (month, day)

SMART Goal:_____

Action Steps:_____

_____

_____

27. SMART Goal:_____

28. Action Steps:_____

_____

_____

SMART Goal:_____

Action Steps:_____

_____

_____

SMART Goal:_____

Action Steps:_____

_____

_____

SMART Goal:_____

Action Steps:_____

_____

_____

SMART Goal:_____

Action Steps:_____

_____

_____

LIFE SKILLS 101

PRINCIPLES & SKILLS

...FINISH

NOTES

SOURCES

1. Cloud, H. (1992). Boundaries: When to Say Yes, How to Say No to Take Control of Your Life. Zondervan: Grand Rapids, MI.

2. Cloud, H. (2011) Necessary Endings: The Employees, Businesses, and Relationships That All of Us Have to Give Up to Move Forward. HarperBusiness: NY, NY

3. Cordeiro, Wayne. (2010). Leading on Empty: Refilling Your Tank and Renewing Your Passion. Bethany House Publishers: Blomington, MN

4. Fields, D. & Rees, E. (2008). Congratulations You're GIFTED! Discovering Your God-Given Shape to Make a Difference in the World. Zondervan: Grand Rapids, MI

5. Gunelius, S. (2010). Blogging, All-in-one for Dummies. Wiley Publishing: I N

6. Goleman, D. (1995). Emotional Intelligence, Why it can matter more than IQ. Bantam Books: NY, NY

7. Harvard School of Public Health: The Nutrition Source. www.hsph.harvard.edu/nutritionsource

8. Halvorson Grant, H. (2011). 9 Things successful people do differently. Harvard Business Review. Boston: MA

9. Holy Bible (1611). King James Version

10. Hyatt, M. (2011). Creating Your Personal Life Plan: A Step-by-Step Guide for Designing the Life You're Always Wanted. Version 1.3, (www.michaelhyatt.com)

11. Hyatt, M. (2013). The Beginner's Guide to Goal Setting. www.michaelhyatt.com

12. McDowel, J. & McDowel, S. (2011). The Unshakable Truth: How You Can Experience the

13. Essentials of a Relevant Faith. Harvest House Publishers: Irvine, CA

14. Meyers, J. (2007). 100 ways to Simplify your life. Faithworks: NY, NY

15. Ramsey, D. (2002) Financial Peace Revisited. Viking Adult:

16. Swenson, R. (2004). Margin: Restoring Emotional, Physical, Financial, and Time Reserves to Overloaded Lives. Navigation Press: Colorado

17. Uhlenberg, B. & Estrem, C. (1988). *Life Skills for Single Parents: A Curriculum Guide.* ERIC Documents (ED326642, CE 056371)

18. www.cashcourse.org

19. www.claudiosantori.it.com

20. www.entrepeneur.com

21. www.heartpoint.com

22. www.investopedia.com

23. www.legal-dictionary.thefreedictionary.com

24. www.merriamwebster.com www.michaelhyatt.com

25. www.myfitnesspal.com

26. www.worldlifeexpectancy.com

27. http://www.ogforlife.com/wp-content/uploads/2014/11/FoodPyramid

28. http://enrichmentjournal.ag.org/201202/201202_028_Biblical_foundations.cfm.gif

29. http://www.christiahttp://waterbrookmultnomah.com/pdf/LAZStudyLeadersGuide. pdfnitytoday.com/iyf/hottopics/friendsfamily/good-friend-bad-friend.html

30. Hyatt, M. & Harkavy, D (2016). *Living Forward: A proven plan to stop drifting and get the life you want.* Baker books: Grand Rapids, MI.

31. Burns, J (2010). *Teenology: The Art of Raising Great Teenagers.* Bethany House: Minneapolis, Minnesota.

32. Meyers, J (2006). *Battlefield of the Mind for Teens: Winning the battle in your mind.* Warner Faith: New York, NY

33. Stanley, A (2011). *Guardrails: Avoiding Regrets in your life.* Zondervan: Grand Rapids, MI.

34. Rath, T (2013). *Eat Move Sleep: how small choices lead to big changes.* MissionDay

35. Sutherland, D & Nowery, K (2003). *The 33 laws of Stewardship: Principles for a life of true fulfillment.* Spire Resources Inc: Camarillo, CA

36. Jones, B & Powell, T (2000). *Discovering your Identity: Realizing Who you are in Christ.* Christian Publications Inc: Camp Hill, PA

37. McGee, R (1998). *The Search for Significance: We can build our self-worth on our ability to please others or on the love and forgiveness of Jesus Christ.* W Publishing Group: Nashville, TN

38. Hybels, B (2002). *Courageous Leadership.* Zondervan: Grand Rapids, MI.

39. Fields, D & Rees, E (2008). *Congratulations you are gifted: Discovering your God-given shape to make a difference in the world.* Zondervan: Grand Rapids, MI

40. Rees. E (2006). *S.H.A.P.E (finding and fulfilling your unique purpose for life).* Zondervan: Grand Rapids, MI

41. Cloud, H (1992). *Changes that heal: How to understand your past to ensure a healthier Future.* Zondervan: Grand Rapids, MI

42. Duhigg, C (2012). *The Power of Habit: Why we do what we do in life and business.* Random House Inc: New York, NY

43. Pozen, R (2012). *Extreme Productivity: Boost your results, Reduce your hours.* Harper Collins Publishers: New York, NY

44. Covey, S (1989). *The seven habits of highly effective people.* Free Press: New York, NY

45. Mckeown, G (2014). *Essentialism: The disciplined pursuit of less.* The Crown Publishing Group/Penguin Random House: New York, NY

46. http://auto.howstuffworks.com/auto-racing/motorsports/formula-one.htm

47. http://auto.howstuffworks.com/auto-racing/nascar

48. https://en.wikipedia.org/wiki/Formula_One

49. http://abundance.ca/wp-content/uploads/2014/10/Money_Matters_for_Youth.pdf

50. https://www.psychologytoday.com/basics/self-esteem

51. Scazzero, P (2011). *Emotionally Healthy Spirituality: Unleash a Revolution in Your Life In Christ.* Thomas Nelson: Nashville, TN

52. Bach, D (2003). *The Finish Rich Workbook: Get out of debt, put your dreams in action and achieve financial freedom.* Broadway Books: New York, NY

53. *Merrill, R & Merrill, R (2004). Life Matters: Creating a dynamic balance of work, family, time and money. McGraw Hill Education: New York, NY*

54. *https://en.wikipedia.org/wiki/Auto_racing*

55. *http://articles.latimes.com/1985-05-19/sports/sp-9410_1_race-drivers*

56. *Elrod, H (2012). The Miracle Morning: The Not-So-Obvious Secret Guaranteed to Transform Your Life (Before 8 AM). Hal Elrod,*

57. *Beckles, C (), Training a Godly Seed. Cedric Beckles*

58. *http://www.makeitcountonline.ca/msc/parents/pdf/msc-make-it-count-parent-eng.pdf*

59. *https://en.wikipedia.org/wiki/Pit_stop*

60. *http://lancasteronline.com/features/big-picture-pit-crews-play-important-role-in-nascar/article_3e497721-a502-5e17-abee-8cecbfc2ecff.html*

61. *https://guides.wikinut.com/NASCAR%   3A-Why-a-good-pit-crew-is-important/1gx55sxj/*

62. *Furtick, S (2015).Crash the Chatterbox: Hearing God's Voice Above All Others. Multnomah: Colorado Springs, CO*

63. *Shirer, P (2015). Fervent: A woman's battle plan for serious, specific and strategic prayer. B&H Publishing Group: Nashville, TN*

64. *Stevenson, S (2016). Sleep Smarter: 21 Essential Strategies to Sleep Your Way to A Better Body, Better Health, and Bigger Success. Rodale Books: Emmaus, Pennsylvania*

65. *https://www.fastcompany.com/3027809/7-time-management-strategies-from-some-brilliant-teenage-prodigies*

66. *https://www.slideshare.net/HassanShahzad2/maslows-hierarchy-of-needs-52444959*

67. *http://www.character-training.com/blog/*

68. *https://www.mindtools.com/pages/article/newTED_85.htm*

69. *http://dictionary.cambridge.org/dictionary/english/discipline*

70. *Stanley, A (2011). Guardrails: Avoiding the regrets in your life. Zondervan: Grand Rapids, MI*

71. *https://www.bible.com/bible/1/2SA.7.22*

72. *http://www.dictionary.com/browse/god*

73. *https://www.google.bs/search?q=vince+lombardi&rlz=1C1CHZL_enBS691BS69
1&oq=vince+lom&aqs=chrome.0.0l2j69i57j0l3.3735j0j9&sourceid=chrome&ie=
UTF-8#q=paul+in+the+bible*

74. *https://www.google.bs/search?q=vince+lombardi&rlz=1C1CHZL_enBS691BS691&oq=
vince+lom&aqs=chrome.0.0l2j69i57j0l3.3735j0j9&sourceid=chrome&ie=UTF-8*

75. *https://www.google.bs/search?q=what+is+the+best+selling+book+of+all+time&rlz
=1C1CHZL_enBS691BS691&oq=what+is+the+best+selling+boo&aqs=chro
me.0.0j69i57j0l4.18400j0j1&sourceid=chrome&ie=UTF-8*

76. *http://biblereasons.com/bible-facts/*

77. *Wilkinson, B & Woods, L & Kirk, Paula (1991,2003). Youth Walk: NIV Walk Thru the
Bible. Zondervan: Grand Rapids, MI*

78. *Richards, L (2001). Every Name of God in the Bible. Thomas Nelson Publishers:
Nashville, TN*

79. *http://biblehub.com/romans/10-9.htm*

80. *http://www.azquotes.com/quote/735462*

Printed in the United States
By Bookmasters